The Bedtime Book of
Animals

Take a peek at more than **100** of your favorite animals

Written by: Zeshan Akhter
Illustrated by: Jean Claude, Livi Gosling,
Kaja Kajfez, Charlotte Milner, Marc Pattenden,
Sandhya Prabhat, Kate Slater, Sara Ugolotti

Contents

Mammals

Fox

Mammals either have **fur** or **hair**. Babies drink their mother's **milk**.

Reptiles

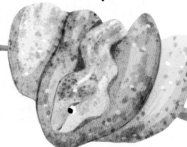

Snake

Reptiles have **scales** or hard **plates** on their bodies. Most lay **eggs**.

Fish

Shark

Fish live in water and have **gills**. Most have **scales** and **fins**.

Tree of life

The tree of life shows how all living things are **related** to each other. It puts animals that are like one another into different groups.

Birds

Birds have two **wings**, a **beak**, and two **clawed feet**.

Parrot

Amphibians

Amphibians have **smooth skin** with no scales, hair, or feathers.

Frog

Invertebrates

Jellyfish

Invertebrates **do not have skeletons** inside their bodies.

Bee

All animals that are not invertebrates are **vertebrates**. This means that they have a **backbone**.

Nine out of ten animals are invertebrates.

Habitats

Habitats are places where animals live. There are many different habitats all over the world. An animal's habitat is the **best place** for it.

Mountain

Some animals live high in the mountains, often in harsh weather.

Forest

These tree-filled places can be woodlands or rainforests.

Polar

Polar habitats are
cold, snowy, and
surrounded by
icy seas.

Ocean

Oceans are huge
areas of salty
water that cover
much of our
planet.

Grassland

These wide-open
spaces are covered
by grass and
sometimes flowers.

Desert

Deserts are hot
or cold places
where not much
rain falls.

Food chains

A food chain is the story of how living things get **energy** from the food they eat. Whether eating or being eaten, all animals are part of a food chain.

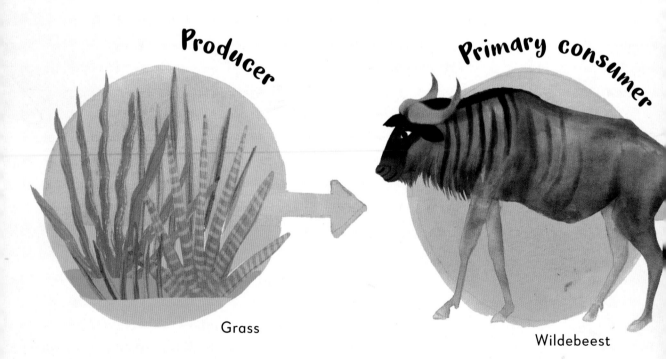

Producer

Grass

Primary consumer

Wildebeest

A producer **makes its own food** using sunlight and water.

Primary consumers cannot make their own food. They eat **plants**.

Animal diets

There are three main groups of animals based on their diet. Carnivores eat meat, herbivores eat plants, and omnivores eat both.

Carnivore   **Herbivore**   **Omnivore**

Secondary consumer

Lion

These **predators** catch and eat primary consumers as **prey**.

Decomposer

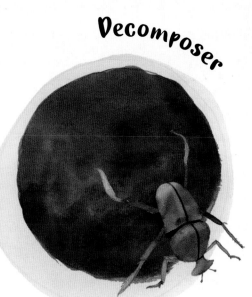

Dung beetle

Decomposers eat animal **poop** and **dead** plants and animals.

Mammals

From mini mice to whopping whales,
mammals can be found roaming the land
or swimming in the oceans. All mammals
have hair, whether it's a little or a lot!

Big cats

These are no ordinary cats. They are much larger, and they are also some of the **fastest** and **strongest** animals in the world.

Striped fur

Tigers are the **largest** and **strongest** of all cats.

Each **paw** has sharp **claws**.

Tiger

Grown-up male lions have a thick, shaggy **mane**.

Lions live in groups called **prides**.

Lions sleep up to twenty hours a day.

Lion

Stubby tail

Pointy ears

The bobcat can **climb** trees.

Bobcat

The spotted **cheetah** is the fastest animal on Earth. It can run three times faster than any human.

Cheetah

Strong legs

This big cat can live in jungles and deserts.

Some big cats **roar** to scare enemies away. Other cats can only purr instead.

Puma

More big cats

Most big cats usually live **alone**, except mothers taking care of their **cubs**.

Leopard spots are called **rosettes**.

Spotted fur helps leopards to hide in the grass.

Leopard

Whiskers

Snow leopard

The **stealthy** snow leopard is known as the "ghost of the mountains."

Snow leopards live on cold mountain slopes.

Jaguars can be spotted or plain black.

Jaguar

Climbing trees helps jaguars find prey.

Big cats have excellent **eyesight** and can move very **quietly**. They often hunt at night, when they can sneak up on prey and pounce.

Big cats like to stretch, especially after sleeping.

Black panther

Big, sharp teeth

15

Cat

Black or white, spotted or striped, there are many types of small cats. These adorable animals make good **pets**, because they can be soft, cuddly, and playful.

Most cats have twelve **whiskers** on each cheek.

Spotted coat

Bengal cat

Striped fur

Cat **paws** are very sensitive. They can feel tiny objects.

Tabby cat

Cats have sharp **hearing** and especially excellent **eyesight**. They can see very well in the dark.

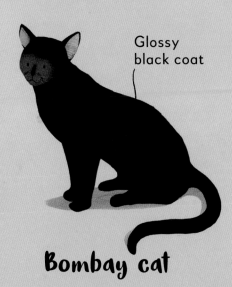

Glossy black coat

Bombay cat

Pale fur coat

Dark tail

Siamese cat

Long white hair

Bushy tail

Persian cat

Short, thick fur

British shorthair cat

Cats purr when they are feeling happy and calm. **Meow!**

Dog

Long, thick coat for warmth

Golden fur

Labrador

Long, narrow body

Short legs

Dachshund

Sheepdog

Dogs of all shapes and sizes love going for **walks**, eating treats, playing with toys, and being petted.

Many dogs can make
wonderful pets because
they are friendly and
cuddly. They are very
loyal animals.

Soft,
fluffy fur

Collie

White fur with
black spots

Dalmatian

Greyhounds are
the **fastest** dogs
in the world.

Slender
body

Greyhound

These clever creatures talk to each
other by **barking**. Woof woof!

Wolf

Wolves live in groups called packs.
They **howl** to talk to one another.
These eerie calls are very loud, so they
can be heard a long way away.

Hooowl!

Wolves often
hunt at **night**.

Wolves have
two layers of
fur to keep
them warm.

White fur helps
the Arctic wolf
stay hidden in
the snow.

20

The **Fennec fox** is very small, but has large ears.

Most foxes have long, bushy tails.

Fox

Foxes hunt for food at night. They have fantastic **hearing**, sharp eyesight, and a super sense of smell.

Dingo

Dingoes are dog-like animals that live in many parts of Australia. They are fast runners, **high jumpers**, and excellent diggers.

Pointy ears

Dingoes can leap up more than twice their own height!

White paws

Thick, waterproof fur keeps sea otters warm.

Sea otters dive deep underwater to find food to eat.

Sea otter

These furry swimmers live in the ocean.
They like to **float** on their back and nap in the sun.
Sometimes, they **smash** shells with rocks
to get the food inside.

Sea otters love to munch on sea urchins.

22

Badger

Badgers burrow underground to dig out dens, called **setts**. They put grass in these homes to make them cozy.

Badgers can't see very well, so they use their **ears** and **nose** to find their way around.

Sniff, sniff, snuffle

Watch out! Skunks can **squirt** a smelly liquid from their butt.

Skunk

Striped skunks eat almost **anything**. They'll even root around in garbage to find food.

Long whiskers

These long teeth are called **tusks**.

Walruses have four flippers.

Under the skin is a layer of fat called **blubber**. It keeps the walrus warm.

Walrus

It's hard work being a walrus. They go swimming to find food in the freezing cold sea, then use their **flippers** and **tusks** to haul themselves out.

Seal

Thick fur keeps seals warm.

Seals dive deep into the icy water, looking for fish to eat. It's a good thing they can hold their breath for up to half an hour!

When they're not swimming, they like lying on rocks and basking in the sun.

Whiskers help animals to sense what is around them.

25

Brown bear

Brown bears sleep through the winter, snuggling up in warm, cozy dens. This is called **hibernation**. When they wake up, they feast on plants and fish.

Round ears

Black nose

Thick fur keeps brown bears warm all year around.

Brown bears use their claws to dig dens.

Sharp **claws** on each paw

Fur blends in with the white snow.

A baby polar bear is called a **cub**.

Claws help polar bears grip slippery ice and catch seals.

Polar bear

These huge beasts live near icy seas in the **freezing** far north of our planet called the Arctic. Underneath their dazzling fur, the skin is black.

Giant panda

The giant panda's favorite food is **bamboo**, so of course they choose to live in bamboo forests! These chunky **bears** eat it almost all day long.

Chomp, chomp

Round, black ears

Black rings around eyes

Sharp teeth cut through tough bamboo.

Claws

Small
ears

Orange-colored
fur

Bushy
tail

Whiskers

Red pandas live in forests high up in the mountains.

Red panda

Red pandas spend most of their time in
trees. They use their long, striped tails to
balance while scurrying around on branches.

Rhinoceros

Rhinoceroses, or rhinos for short, live in hot places. They cool off by wallowing in **mud baths**. The mud stops their skin from burning in the sun.

Thick, gray skin

Rhinos are very big and powerful, and they can get very angry. When they fight, they use their **nose horn** as a weapon.

Rhinos are the second largest land animals.

A baby rhino is called a **calf**.

Rhinos only eat grass and other plants.

Horse

Horses are strong, powerful, and can run at great speeds. Each one has a hairy **mane**, a long **tail**, and hard **hooves** on its feet.

The **mane** grows on the top of the neck.

Small horses like this one are called **ponies**.

Shetland pony

Hoof

Horses swish their **tails** to swat away insects.

Horses can **walk** slowly, **trot** a little faster, **canter** briskly, or **gallop** at full speed.

Horse

Zebra

At first glance, horse-like zebras might all look the same, but each one has its own unique pattern of black and white **stripes** on its fur.

Zebras like to eat **grass**.

Hoof

Strong, sturdy body

Short, tufted tail

Zebras graze and play under the hot sun in Africa.

Yak

Yaks live high up in cold mountains where there is not much air. They have big **lungs** that help them breathe. Yaks love to eat grass. They travel great distances to find it.

A woolly, waterproof coat keeps yaks warm and dry.

Long horns

Long tail

Hooves

Yaks use their horns to move snow to look for food.

34

Deer

Deer roam woodlands to find leaves, shrubs, and grasses to eat. Male deer have **antlers**, which fall off in winter but grow back again each spring.

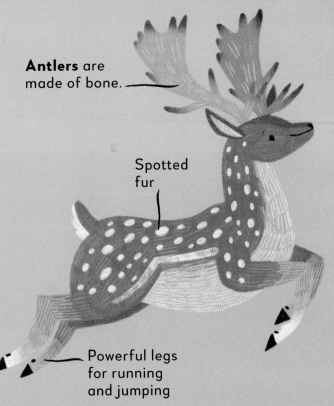

Antlers are made of bone.

Spotted fur

Powerful legs for running and jumping

Moose

Large antlers **impress** other deer.

Short tail

Hefty, hairy moose are the **largest** type of deer. Surprisingly, they can swim!

This flap of hairy skin is called a **dewlap**.

Thick body hair

Buffalo

There can be **thousands** of sturdy buffalo in a single herd. Their strength in numbers helps to keep them safe from unfriendly animals!

A buffalo's horns grow right across its head.

Curved horns

Droopy ears

Cow

Cows are **calm**, sturdy animals. They often live in groups and spend most of their time eating grass.

Straight back

Moo!

A cow's stomach has **four** sections that help break down food.

Udders make milk to feed baby cows, or calves.

Thick, curly **fleece**

Baa!

Sheep

These woolly bundles are often found grazing in fields. They live in groups called **flocks**.

Camel

The **hump** stores fat that the camel can live off of for weeks.

Two layers of long **eyelashes** keep out sand and dust.

A camel can drink a whole **bathtub** of water at once!

Camels live in hot, dry **deserts**. Luckily, they can last a long time between drinks. Their long, knobbly legs are very strong.

A giraffe's tongue is dark and **sticky**.

Giraffe

Giraffes are the **tallest** animals in the whole wide world. Some are taller than a house! They live in Africa.

These bony points are called **ossicones**.

Giraffes have **three hearts**.

Golden fur with large brown patches

Having such a **long** neck is useful for reaching tasty leaves high up on trees.

Alpaca

Alpacas, vicuñas, and llamas all live in the mountains of **South America**.

Alpaca hair can be made into woolly sweaters.

Alpacas mostly eat grass.

Stocky body shape

Alpacas do not live in the wild. They are taken care of by farmers and live together in groups called **herds**. They look cuddly, but watch out for their kick!

Vicuña

Vicuñas roam free high up on the mountainside. They are fast runners with fine, soft fur.

Slender legs

Long, curved ears

Llama

Llamas are strong and can balance on steep hills. In their rocky homelands, they often help people carry things.

Whale

These mighty sea creatures are record-breaking **divers**. Some whales can hold their breath for up to an hour!

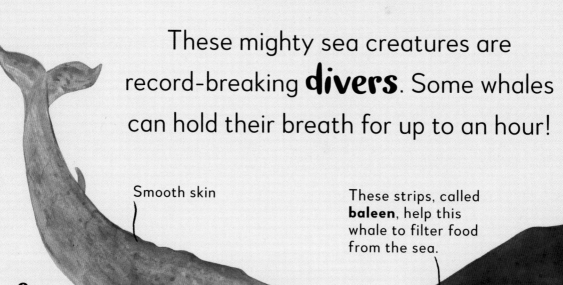

Smooth skin

These strips, called **baleen**, help this whale to filter food from the sea.

Gray whale

Blue whale

Whales talk using clicks, whistles, and musical calls.

Long **flippers** for speedy swimming

Humpback whale

Minke whale

White belly

Swishing tail fins power whales through the water.

Whales live in groups called pods.

The blue whale is the **largest** animal on Earth. It is as long as an airplane!

Whales come to the surface to breathe through **blowholes** on their backs.

The **dorsal fin** is on the whale's back. It helps with balance.

Sperm whale

Small, beady eyes

Dolphins are very fast swimmers.

Dolphins breathe through their **blowhole**.

Tail fin, called a **fluke**

Flipper

Common dolphin

Dolphin

Dolphins are clever and playful. They travel together in **pods**, talk to each other in clicks and whistles, and like to leap out of the sea.

Dorsal fin for balance

The orca is the **largest** dolphin. It can weigh more than three cars!

Smooth skin

Orca

Narwhal

Narwhals live in freezing seawater surrounded by ice. The long spike on their head is called a **tusk**, which is a type of tooth.

A narwhal's **tusk** can grow to be longer than a grown-up human!

Tail fin

Narwhals are nicknamed "unicorns of the sea."

Hippopotamus

Hefty hippopotamuses spend most of their day relaxing in water. This keeps them cool in the **heat**, since it is very warm in their grassland homes.

Thick skin

These plant-eaters love to eat grass.

Grunt grunt!

Honk honk!

46

Hippos are very **protective** of their families. They will use their teeth as a weapon if they are in danger.

A group of hippopotamuses is called a bloat.

A hippopotamus has almost **no hair** on its body.

A baby hippopotamus is called a calf.

Huge teeth look a little bit like tusks.

Bat

Bats are the only mammals that can **fly**. They come out at night to find food.

Thumb-like claw

Fur around eyes looks like glasses.

Spectacled flying fox

Wide wings for fast flight

Egyptian fruit bat

Megabats are some of the biggest bats in the world. They eat fruit, nectar, or pollen.

Eastern tube-nosed bat

Long, tube-like nostrils

Many bats use sound to find their food. This is called echolocation.

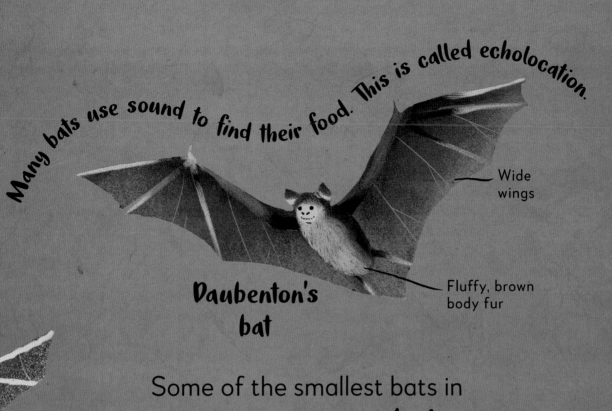

Wide wings

Fluffy, brown body fur

Daubenton's bat

Some of the smallest bats in the world are **microbats**. They mostly eat insects.

Yellow wings

Gray fur on body

Yellow-winged bat

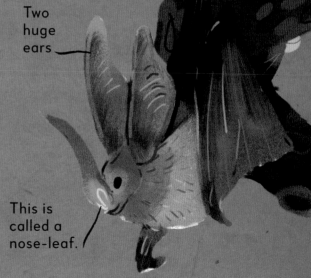

Two huge ears

This is called a nose-leaf.

Sword-nosed bat

Hedgehog

A hedgehog curls up into a ball if it is scared.

Pointy spikes,
called **quills**

Hedgehogs are small,
spiky animals. They
sleep during the day
and come out at night
to find food.

Long **snout**
for sniffing
out food

Hedgehogs like
to eat **berries**,
but look for beetles
and caterpillars to
chomp on, too.

Paws with long, sharp claws

Dig dig dig dig

Mole

Moles are really good at **digging**!
Their powerful front paws work like spades.
They carve out long tunnels and make
homes underground.

Rabbit

Rabbits live in underground homes called burrows. Above ground, they **hop** from place to place, nibbling on plants as they go.

Some kinds of rabbits are sweet and cuddly and make excellent **pets**.

Round, fluffy tail

Long ears

Soft fur

Whiskers

Rabbits have teeth and nails that never stop growing.

52

Hare

Like rabbits, hares have good **hearing**.

Snowshoe hare

Big feet help this hare balance on snow and ice.

Sometimes hares need to escape predators. Luckily, they can run extremely **fast**.

Huge ears

Hares are **larger** than rabbits.

Hares have long, strong back legs, helping them to **bound** quickly across the ground.

American desert hare

53

Rodents

Small, furry rodents are found almost everywhere in the world. They gnaw on food with sharp, pointy **teeth** that never stop growing!

Capybaras are the **largest** rodents. They are very friendly animals.

Capybara

Pygmy jerboa

This is the **smallest** of all rodents. It hops to move around.

Whiskers

Tiny mice can **jump**, **climb**, and even **swim**.

Mouse

Beavers build homes from branches, twigs, and mud.

A beaver's tail
looks sort of
like a paddle.

Beaver

Some rodents live alone, but many live in groups. These groups have underground homes near one another called **towns**.

Guinea pigs don't
have **tails**.

Guinea pig

Feet on very
short legs

Gorilla

Gorillas have thick, black hair.

Gorilla families live together in the beautiful forests of Africa.

Strong, muscular legs

Gorillas can feel happy and sad, just like humans.

Boom, boom! Gorillas **beat** their chests to show how big and strong they are, but they are gentle giants. They are very happy eating leaves.

Orangutan

Orangutans are part of a family of animals called the great apes, which also includes gorillas—and humans!

Strong arms

Orangutans are natural **acrobats**. They swing from tree to tree with ease.

Tight grip

These great apes are very **smart**. They use tools to do things, and make impressive nests.

Monkey

There are hundreds of different types of monkeys that live all over the world. Monkeys can **swing** between tree branches to get from place to place.

Ooh aah aah!

Its face gets even brighter when it is **excited**.

The mandrill is the **largest** of all monkeys.

Hair grows around its colorful face, but not on it.

Mandrill

Some monkeys like to stay **high** up in trees, but others come down and scamper around on the forest floor.

Vervet monkey

Monkeys like to eat fruit, leaves, nuts, and insects. Young monkeys love to **play**!

Golden snub-nosed monkey

Monkeys live in groups called **troops**.

Golden marmoset

Sloth

Sloths live in trees in rainforests. They eat twigs and leaves. Sloths move slowly and spend most of their day **sleeping**.

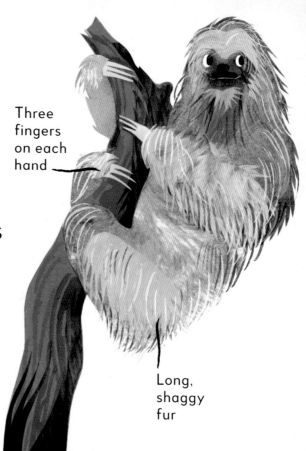

Three fingers on each hand

Long, shaggy fur

Anteaters eat thousands of insects every day!

White stripe

Thick, brown fur

Armadillo

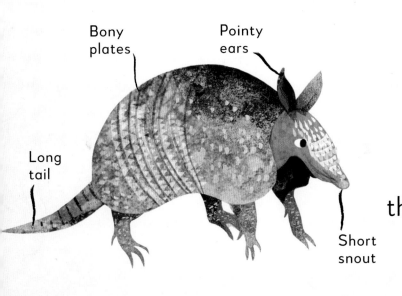

Bony plates

Pointy ears

Long tail

Short snout

Armadillos are covered in hard, bony plates. This **armor** protects them from predators.

Anteater

Thin tongue

Anteaters do not have teeth. To eat, they poke their snouts into ant nests and scoop the insects out with their **sticky** tongues.

Elephant

Elephants can live in many different places, from lush wetlands and forests to sparse savannas and deserts. Wherever they **roam**, elephants take great care of each other.

Big, flapped ears

Long, curved tusks

Strong legs

62

An elephant's trunk is actually a long nose. Elephants use it to smell, to grab plants to eat, and even as a **snorkel** when swimming.

Elephants live and travel in family groups called herds.

Thick, gray skin

A baby elephant is called a calf.

Marsupials

Hairy marsupials come in many shapes and sizes. Most live in dry **deserts**, but some make their home in woodlands and rainforests.

Small, compact body shape

This baby koala is nestled in its mother's pouch.

Koala

Wombat

Whiskers

All baby marsupials are called joeys.

Strong legs for hopping around

Kangaroo

Opossums sometimes carry their babies on their backs.

Opossum

Large, pointed ears

Wallabies look similar to kangaroos, but are smaller.

Long, furry tail

Wallaby

Scattering of white spots on fur

Quoll

Small, round ears

A quokka is around the size of a cat.

Quokka

Mommy marsupials have a special **pouch** on their tummy. Inside, their tiny babies grow and get ready to explore.

Platypus

A platypus has a duck-like bill and a tail like a beaver. These animals hunt for food underwater. Platypuses are one of only two mammals that **lay eggs**.

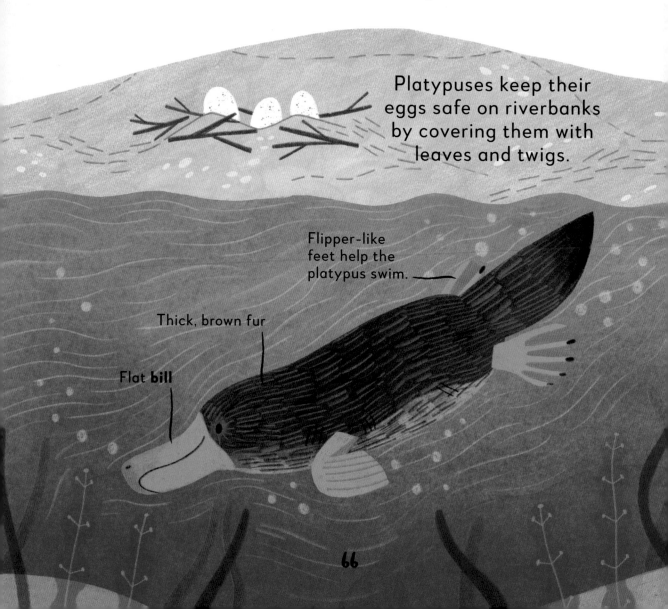

Platypuses keep their eggs safe on riverbanks by covering them with leaves and twigs.

Flipper-like feet help the platypus swim. ——

Thick, brown fur

Flat **bill**

Echidna

Echidnas lay eggs instead of giving birth to live young. They lay one at a time. Each echidna egg hatches into a baby called a **puggle**.

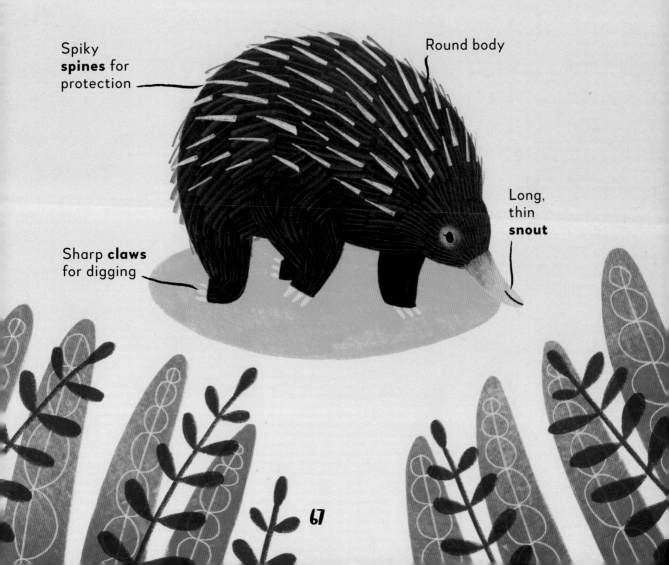

Spiky **spines** for protection

Round body

Long, thin **snout**

Sharp **claws** for digging

Birds

All birds have feathers and two wings, which many use to fly through the skies. These incredible creatures sing, chirp, squawk, and coo to talk to each other.

Songbirds

Thousands of birds make calls that sound **musical**. These birds are known as songbirds. They sing from dawn until dusk.

Superb starling

Painted bunting

Chirp, chirp!

Red belly feathers

Northern red bishop

Orange feathers wrap around the body.

Small, sharp beak

Blue tit

Songbirds can **grip** tightly onto branches. This stops them from dropping to the ground when they fall asleep.

This songbird can have a black, red, or yellow face.

Each songbird sings its own song.

Gouldian finch

Golden-fronted leafbird

This green, leaf-colored bird blends into the trees.

Clawed feet

Blackbird

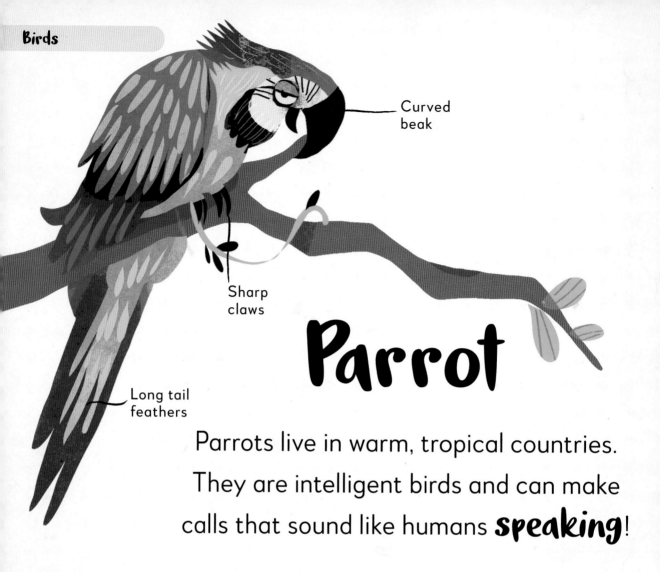

Curved beak

Sharp claws

Long tail feathers

Parrot

Parrots live in warm, tropical countries. They are intelligent birds and can make calls that sound like humans **speaking**!

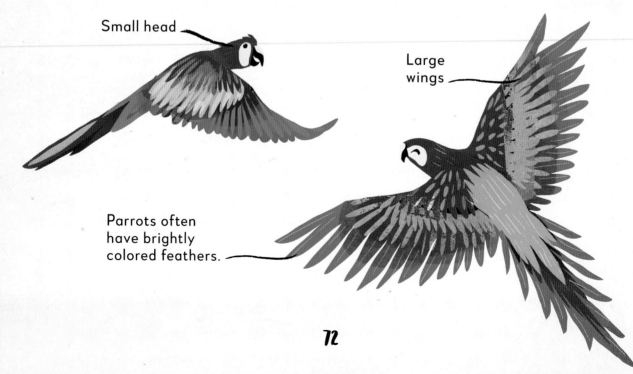

Small head

Large wings

Parrots often have brightly colored feathers.

Squawk!
Cockatoos make a loud, sharp screaming sound. They do this if they are bored, or to warn other cockatoos of danger.

Yellow crest feathers

Cockatoo

Short, sharp beak

Cockatoos are a type of parrot. They are smart, playful, and **noisy**. They love spending time with other cockatoos and live together in flocks.

Wings

This cockatoo is white, but others may have black, gray, or pink feathers.

Toucan

Very strong beak

Small, beady eyes

Black body feathers

Colorful toucans have enormous **beaks**, which can be longer than the rest of their bodies.

This bird hops from tree to tree, making a **croaking** noise to talk to friends.

Woodpecker

Woodpeckers use their tough beaks to **hammer** grooves into tree trunks.

Strong, sharp beak

Stiff tail feathers

Tap tap tap tap tap

They do this to build their **nests** and to find insects to eat.

Kingfisher

Whoosh!

Beautiful blue and orange kingfishers whizz down into quiet streams and rivers, catching fish to eat.

Listen out for a kingfisher's high-pitched call. **"Peep peep!"**

The pointy beak pierces the water very quickly.

Electric blue wing feathers

Kookaburras swoop down on lizards and frogs.

Stripe of gray wing feathers

Short, brown tail feathers

Gray body

Large beak

Kookaburra

You'll hear a kookaburra before you see one. They have a **noisy laugh**, but they are actually very shy. They perch on tree branches in the forests of Australia.

Birds of prey

These awesome creatures are large, strong, and extremely fast flyers. They also have sharp claws and superb eyesight. It is no surprise, then, that they are expert **hunters**.

This is the **largest** bird of prey.

Its huge **wings** stretch out much wider than a grown-up person's arms.

Andean condor

The red kite's forked tail twists gently to keep it **balanced** in flight.

Red kite

Bald eagle

White head feathers

Bald eagles catch fish, snakes, and small mammals.

Peregrine falcon

Large eyes

When it dives through the air, the peregrine falcon travels **faster** than any other animal.

Sharp claws, called **talons**

Vultures feed on **dead** animals.

Bald head

Birds of prey **SWOOP** down to snatch their prey from water, the ground, or even in mid-air.

King vulture

Owl

These birds of prey are **nocturnal**. This means they sleep during the day and are only awake at nighttime.

Snowy owl

Owls can fly **silently** because they have very soft feathers.

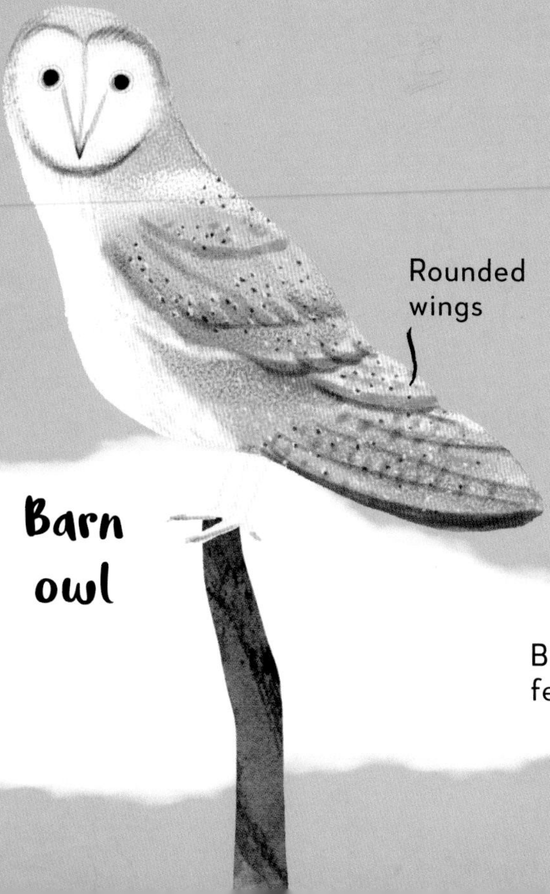

Great horned owl

Rounded wings

Barn owl

Brown feathers

Eagle owls are the biggest owls in the world.

Small, soft feathers on the wing tip

Eagle owl

Elf owl

Huge eyes

These are not real horns! They are feathery tufts.

Short legs

Owls cannot move their eyes left or right. But they can **twist** their heads almost all the way around. This gives them a fantastic all-around view.

Penguin

Most penguins live in frozen Antarctica.
They **waddle** across the ice, or slide
on their bellies.

Yellow
crest

The emperor penguin
is the **largest** penguin
in the world.

**Macaroni
penguin**

Penguin **chicks**
are covered in soft,
fuzzy feathers.

Emperor penguin

White stripe

Black chin feathers

Chinstrap penguin

Gentoo penguin

Penguins have special wings called **flippers**. They use them to swim and dive for their favorite food: fish!

There are eighteen different types of penguins.

A long, sharp **bill** is useful for catching fish.

White ring around eyes

King penguin

Adélie penguin

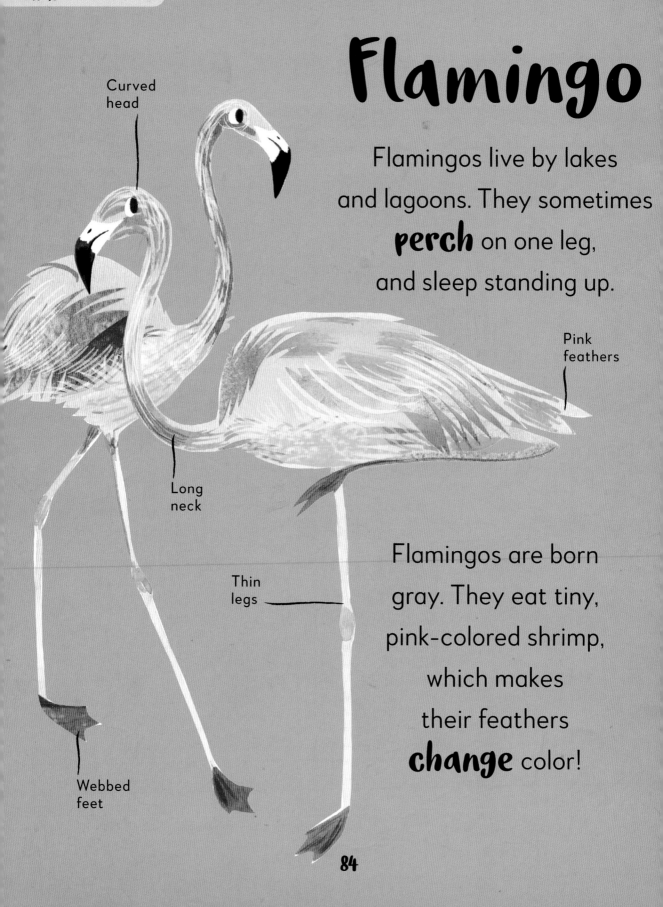

Curved head

Flamingo

Flamingos live by lakes and lagoons. They sometimes **perch** on one leg, and sleep standing up.

Pink feathers

Long neck

Thin legs

Flamingos are born gray. They eat tiny, pink-colored shrimp, which makes their feathers **change** color!

Webbed feet

84

Water birds

Water birds spend most of their time **gliding** along in ponds or resting on riverbanks. They feed on plants, fish, insects, and worms.

Water birds swim by **paddling** their feet through the water.

Long, curved neck

Brown wing feathers

Swan

Duck

Goose

Webbed feet

85

A peacock's tail feathers are called its train.

Each feather has an **eyespot**.

Peacocks spread their feathers to attract peahens.

Peafowl

Male peafowls are called **peacocks** and female peafowls are called **peahens**. Peacocks can have up to 200 brightly colored tail feathers, while peahens are mainly brown.

Chicken

Cluck, cluck! Many chickens live on farms. You might see them strutting around or pecking seeds and bugs from the ground.

Male chickens are called **cockerels**. They call out loudly every morning.

Cock-a-doodle-doo!

Crest

Female chickens are called hens. They lay **eggs** that hatch into baby chicks.

Chickens have **wings**, but they're not very good at flying.

Kiwi

Kiwis have tiny wings, but they are not able to **fly**. Their wings cannot be seen through their feathers.

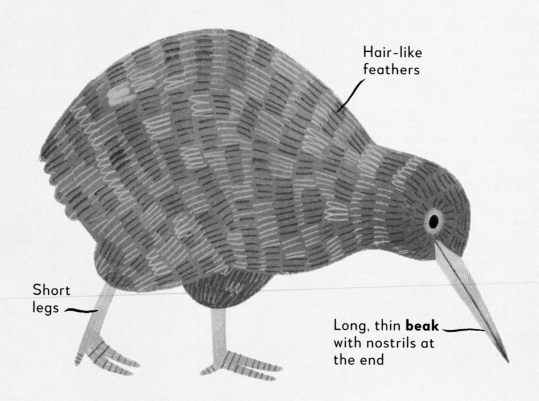

Hair-like feathers

Short legs

Long, thin **beak** with nostrils at the end

Kiwis walk around **sniffing** the ground. They can tell when tasty worms are wriggling underground.

Small beak

Thin, curved neck

This is the only bird with two toes on each foot.

Black and white wing feathers

Long legs

Ostrich

Ostriches live in warm deserts and savannas. They are the biggest birds in the world. Ostriches cannot fly, but they are very fast **runners**.

Reptiles

Reptiles wriggle, slither, swim, and crawl their way across land and water. Many of these cold-blooded animals have colorful, scaly skin.

Crocodile

These powerful predators are the largest reptiles in the world. They can be longer than three grown-up people lying end-to-end!

V-shaped **snout**

Long, sharp **teeth**

Crocodiles have the strongest **bite** of all animals. Snap!

Crocodiles eat fish, birds, and sometimes mammals.

92

Caimans can see well at **night**.

Caiman

Caimans live in rivers, mangroves, swamps, lakes, and marshes. They have strong jaws with a row of **cone-shaped** teeth.

Caimans cannot chew. They **swallow** their food whole.

Alligator

Dark-colored, scaly skin

Alligators have a U-shaped snout.

Alligators can only live in **freshwater** areas, such as rivers and swamps.

Lizard

Lizards are clever creatures. Some can change their skin color, while others can remove their **tails** to escape from a predator's grasp.

Black and white neck stripes

Five toes

Collared lizard

Green **crest** on back

Green basilisk lizard

Striped tail

Zebra-tailed lizard

94

Green
iguana

Curled tail

Toes with
sharp **claws**
for climbing

Iguanas have
sticky tongues,
which they use
to catch flies.

Iguana

Iguanas are a type of lizard. They love to eat insects. Some iguanas can hold their **breath** for up to half an hour when swimming!

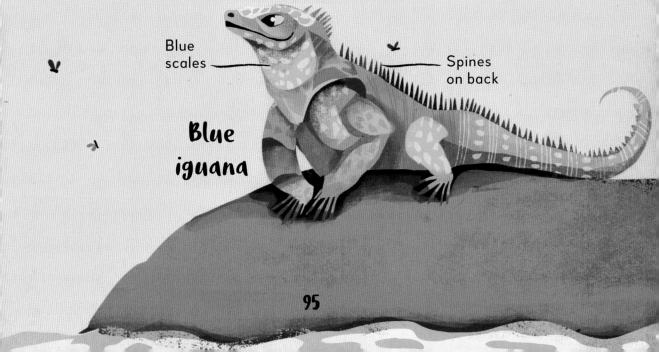

Blue
scales

Spines
on back

Blue
iguana

Chameleon

Chameleons are very colorful lizards. Most chameleons can **change** their skin **color** to blend into their surroundings, or to show how they are feeling.

Some chameleons have **horns** to defend themselves.

If a chameleon is blue or green, it is feeling happy!

Jackson's chameleon

Pygmy chameleon

This is the **smallest** type of chameleon.

96

Panther chameleon

Claws can grip tightly to branches.

A long, curled tail helps with **balance**.

There are more than 150 types of these tree-loving reptiles. They live in warm parts of the world, such as Africa, and they like to eat **insects**.

Meller's chameleon

These **spines** protect the chameleon's back.

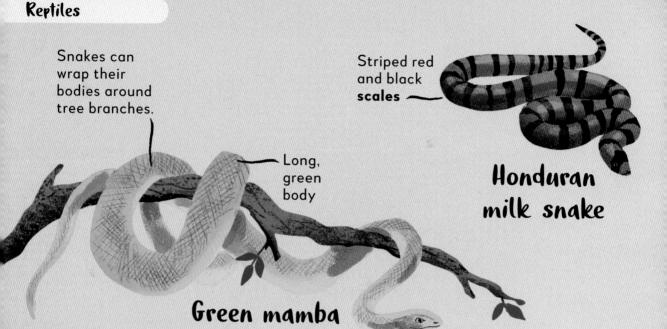

Snakes can wrap their bodies around tree branches.

Long, green body

Striped red and black **scales**

Honduran milk snake

Green mamba

Snake

Snakes can slither around almost **anywhere**. There are even snakes that live in water! Many have sharp teeth and venomous bites.

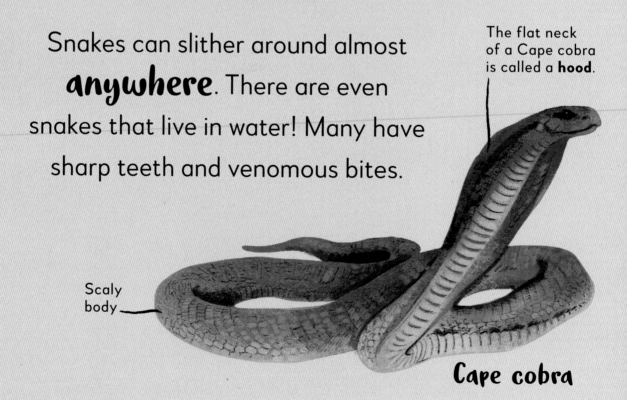

The flat neck of a Cape cobra is called a **hood**.

Scaly body

Cape cobra

Snakes like this one wrap around prey and **squeeze** it.

Small, black eyes

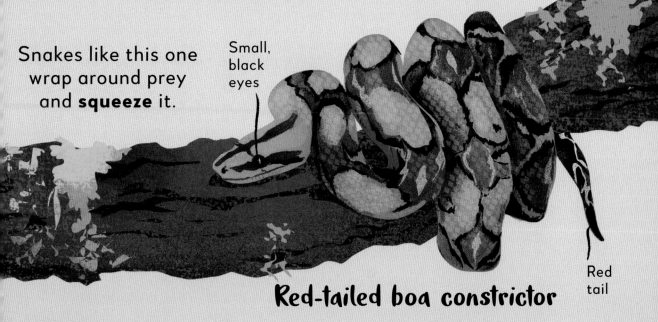

Red-tailed boa constrictor

Red tail

This snake's tail makes a rattling noise when it moves.

Snakes **shed** their skin many times a year. They wriggle out of their old skin, and a fresh new layer takes its place.

Timber rattlesnake

Striped body

Snakes can make a hissing sound when they breathe.

Sidewinder

Slithers sideways when moving.

Forked tongue

Sea turtle

Sea turtles spend most of their time in water and hold their **breath** when diving. Some can stay underwater for up to seven hours while they sleep!

Hard **shell**

Long **flippers**

Baby sea turtles hide in seaweed to avoid being eaten by bigger sea creatures.

Tortoises live for around 150 years.

Large neck

The heavy shell is called a **carapace**.

Clawed feet

Tortoise

Tortoises only live on land. They can pull their head and legs into their safe, strong **shell** to protect themselves from danger.

Amphibians

An amphibian's special talent is that
when it is grown up, it can live on land
and in water. These animals lay eggs,
and many have brightly colored skin.

Toad

Toads can gobble up flies, snails, and slugs
with a lightning fast **flick** of the tongue.
They live in damp places and **crawl** to
ponds and swamps to lay eggs.

Toads make a rattling, rolling noise: "Qwarrk!"

Bumpy,
dry skin

Long,
sticky
tongue

Croak croak!

Large eyes

Short front legs

Sticky pads on toes let tree frogs grip branches.

Tree frog

A frog **croaks** to tell other frogs where it is.

Frog

Frogs use their long back legs to swim and **jump** around. They lay tiny eggs called frogspawn in water. The eggs hatch into babies called **tadpoles**.

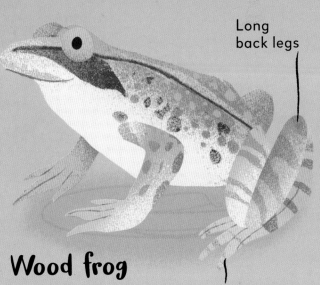

Long back legs

Wood frog

Webbed feet for swimming fast

Salamander

Some salamanders can breathe through their skin.

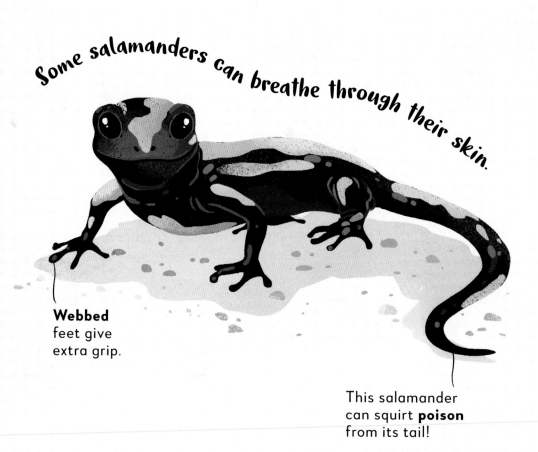

Webbed feet give extra grip.

This salamander can squirt **poison** from its tail!

Salamanders live in cool, wet places. They make their homes under branches, rocks, and leaves. These **slippery** creatures scamper around on all fours looking for food.

Newt

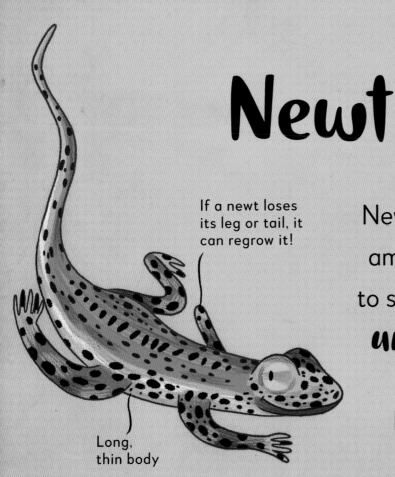

If a newt loses its leg or tail, it can regrow it!

Long, thin body

Newts are small, slimy amphibians that love to swim. Some breathe **underwater**, but others can only breathe on land.

A newt's **skin** can be smooth and wet or dry and bumpy. They like to live in ponds.

Fish

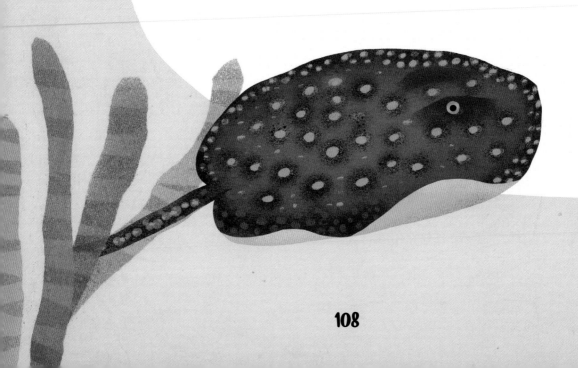

Fish make their homes underwater and use gills in order to breathe. Most fish have scales, smooth bodies, and swishing tails and fins.

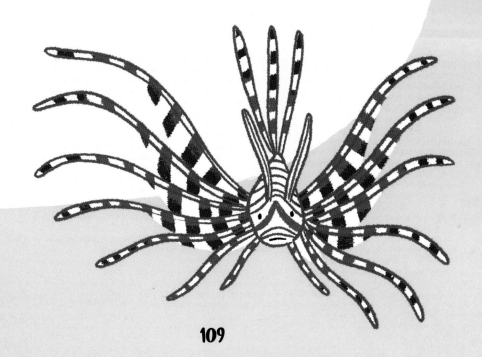

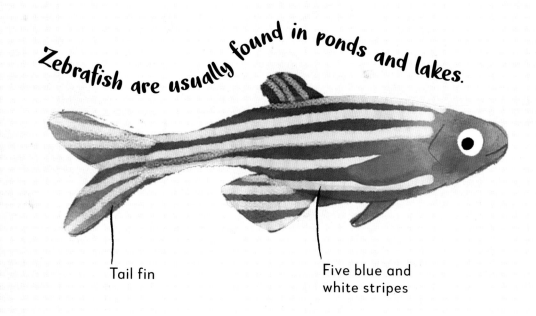

Zebrafish are usually found in ponds and lakes.

Tail fin

Five blue and
white stripes

Zebrafish

These fish are named after zebras because
they have similar **stripes** on their scaly skin.
If they are hurt, zebrafish can regrow
their skin, fins, heart, and brain.

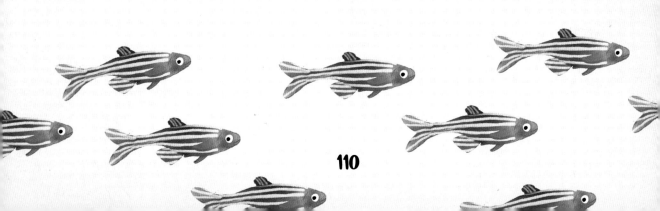

110

Lionfish

Lionfish live in warm waters. The **spines** on their back contain **venom**, which they use to protect themselves from predators. Lionfish are nocturnal, so they are only awake at nighttime.

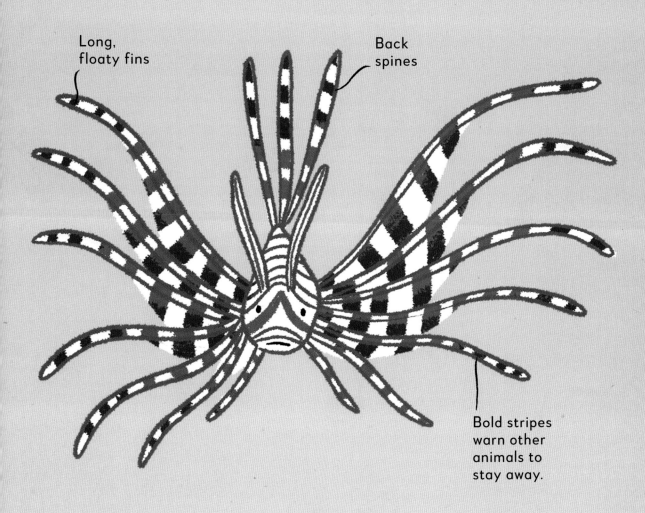

Long, floaty fins

Back spines

Bold stripes warn other animals to stay away.

Seahorse

Seahorses live in shallow sea waters. They swim **upright** and use their back fin to push themselves through the water.

Seahorses **wrap** their curly tails around corals and seaweed to keep from floating away.

The head is shaped like a horse's.

Baby seahorses are called fry.

Tiny, spiny plates cover the entire body.

112

There's one thing that makes these little fish extra special. Unlike every other animal, the daddy seahorse helps the eggs grow into babies in his pouch.

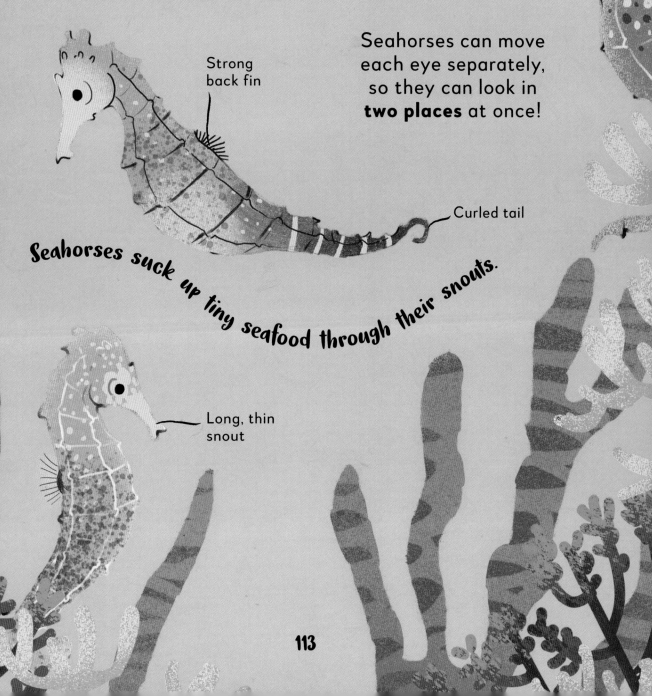

Strong back fin

Seahorses can move each eye separately, so they can look in **two places** at once!

Curled tail

Seahorses suck up tiny seafood through their snouts.

Long, thin snout

X-ray fish live in large groups called shoals.

Striped fins   Bony skeleton

X-ray fish

X-ray fish are almost transparent. You can look right through their **shimmering** scales and see the shape of their backbone and skeleton.

Piranha

Piranhas live in groups in rivers and streams. They have **razor-sharp** teeth that they use to eat insects, other fish, worms, and plants.

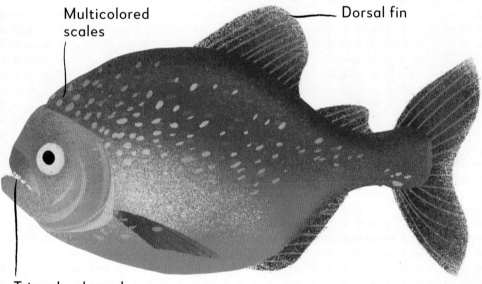

Multicolored scales

Dorsal fin

Triangle-shaped teeth

Piranhas grow several sets of teeth in their lifetime.

Stingray

These disk-shaped creatures use their fins to glide through the water. Stingrays have venomous spikes called **barbs** on their tails, which help them to fight off predators.

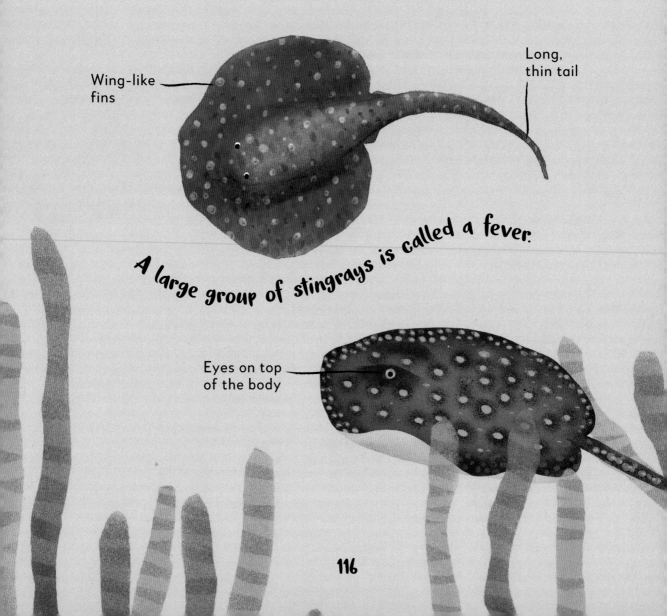

Wing-like fins

Long, thin tail

A large group of stingrays is called a fever.

Eyes on top of the body

Dorsal fin

Up to
300 teeth

Gills for
breathing

Great white
shark

Shark

There are hundreds of types of sharks in the
oceans. Many sharks have a lot of sharp teeth that
they use to **attack** other fish. Their smooth
bodies and powerful fins help them swim fast.

Tiny animals get
caught in the shark's
wide-open **mouth**.

Basking
shark

This **gentle** shark
does not have
big teeth.

Invertebrates

Invertebrates don't have bones, which means they can be squishy, like a slug. However, they can also be spiky, strong, and often strange in interesting ways!

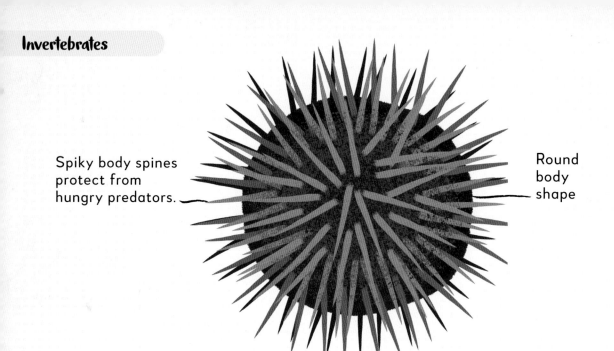

Spiky body spines protect from hungry predators.

Round body shape

Sea urchin

Sea urchins are round and spiky.
They move slowly across the seabed
eating any seaweed in their path.
Underneath their sharp spines
is a hard **shell**.

Sea urchins live by rocks and seaweed.

These creatures often live in groups called herds.

Starfish

Starfish live on the **seabed**. They move around using thousands of tiny feet, which are found under each of their **five** arms.

Spotted orange skin

There is an eye at the end of each arm.

Starfish

Starfish and brittle stars do not have brains.

Round body

The thin arms snap off easily.

Brittle stars are like starfish, but have **thinner** arms.

Brittle star

Flying insects

Believe it or not, these tiny insects are super strong. They need to be, because they beat their wings so hard to stay in the air. That's what makes them **buzz**.

Large eyes

Fly

Flying ants are like normal ants but with wings!

All insects have six legs.

Flying ant

Fuzzy body hair

Bumblebee

These **bees** fly to flowers to drink the **nectar** inside.

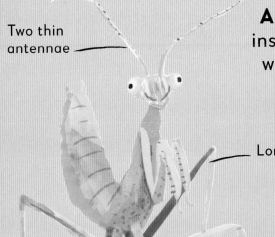

Two thin antennae

Antennae help insects to detect what is around them.

Long legs

Lacy pattern on wings

Praying mantis

Green lacewing

Slender waist

Wasp

Wasps have stingers at the end of their bodies.

There are millions of types of flying insects. Some have a nasty **sting** to defend themselves!

Butterfly

A butterfly starts out life as a **caterpillar**. This tiny bug chomps on leaves, then begins to change form. First it becomes a **chrysalis**, before turning into a fluttering butterfly.

Soft, squishy body

Patterned skin

Caterpillar

Butterflies drink sweet **nectar** from plants and flowers. They have wings with beautiful patterns and can fly.

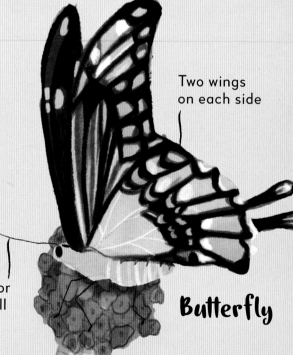

Two wings on each side

Long antennae for balance and smell

Butterfly

124

Dragonfly

Dragonflies are buzzing, acrobatic hunters that can catch flying prey in mid-air. They can zoom straight up and down or **hover** in one place like a helicopter.

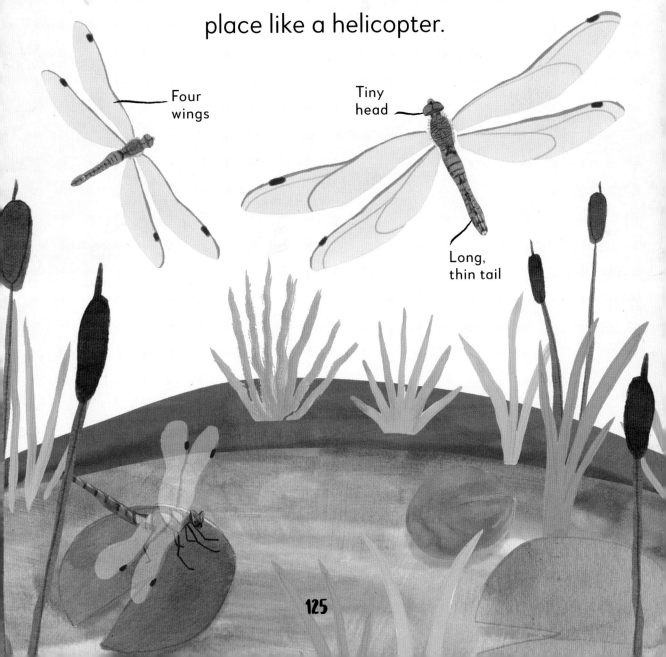

Four wings

Tiny head

Long, thin tail

Beetle

These insects come in all kinds of colors and live in almost every part of the world. They are some of nature's best **cleaners**, because many of them eat up dead plants and animals.

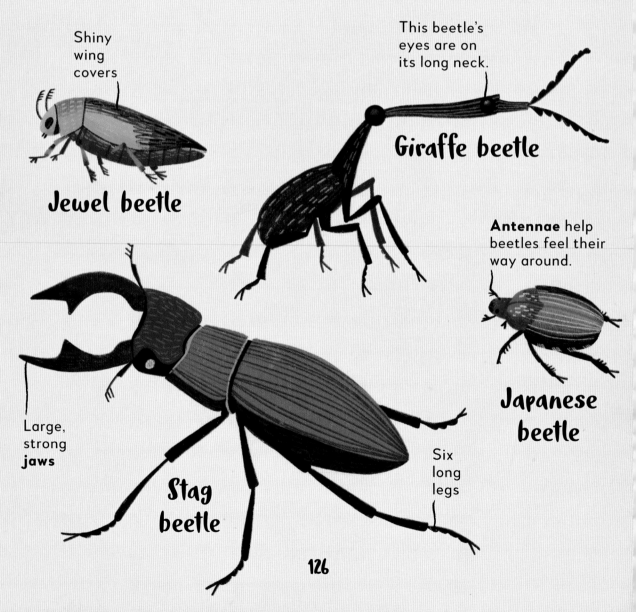

Shiny wing covers

Jewel beetle

This beetle's eyes are on its long neck.

Giraffe beetle

Antennae help beetles feel their way around.

Japanese beetle

Large, strong **jaws**

Stag beetle

Six long legs

126

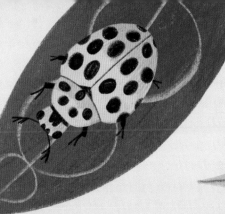

22-spot ladybug

A ladybug's **spots** warn other animals to stay away.

Orange ladybug

Six short legs

Wings are hidden under wing covers.

Two-spot ladybug

Seven-spot ladybug

Two tiny eyes

Cream-spot ladybug

Ladybug

Ladybugs are beetles. There are thousands of different types. Some have **no spots**, while others are covered in them.

Scorpion

Scorpions are small but mighty. They have eight legs and two large pincers. At the end of their tail is a **venomous** stinger.

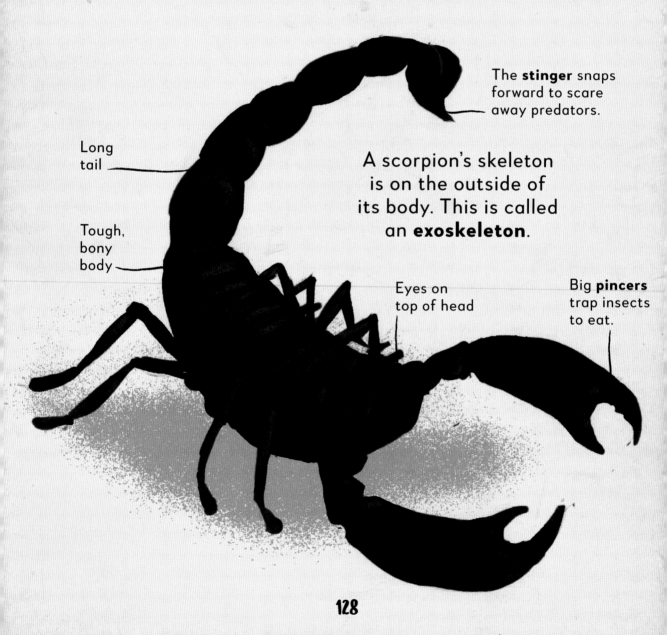

The **stinger** snaps forward to scare away predators.

Long tail

A scorpion's skeleton is on the outside of its body. This is called an **exoskeleton**.

Tough, bony body

Eyes on top of head

Big **pincers** trap insects to eat.

Spider

Spiders come in many different shapes, sizes, and colors. They all have eight legs, many have eight eyes, and some **spin** sticky webs.

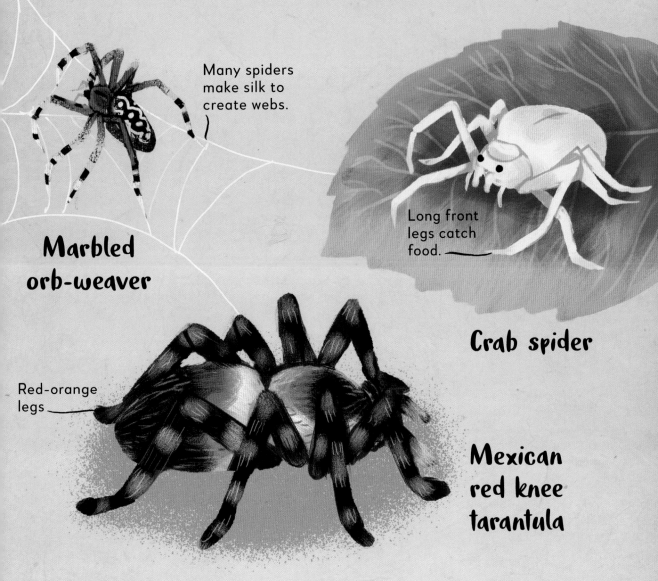

Many spiders make silk to create webs.

Marbled orb-weaver

Long front legs catch food.

Crab spider

Red-orange legs

Mexican red knee tarantula

Crab

Crabs can live on land or in the sea. They use their back legs to **scuttle** sideways on sand. Their two front legs have claws on each end for grabbing food.

Crabs are protected from predators by a hard shell.

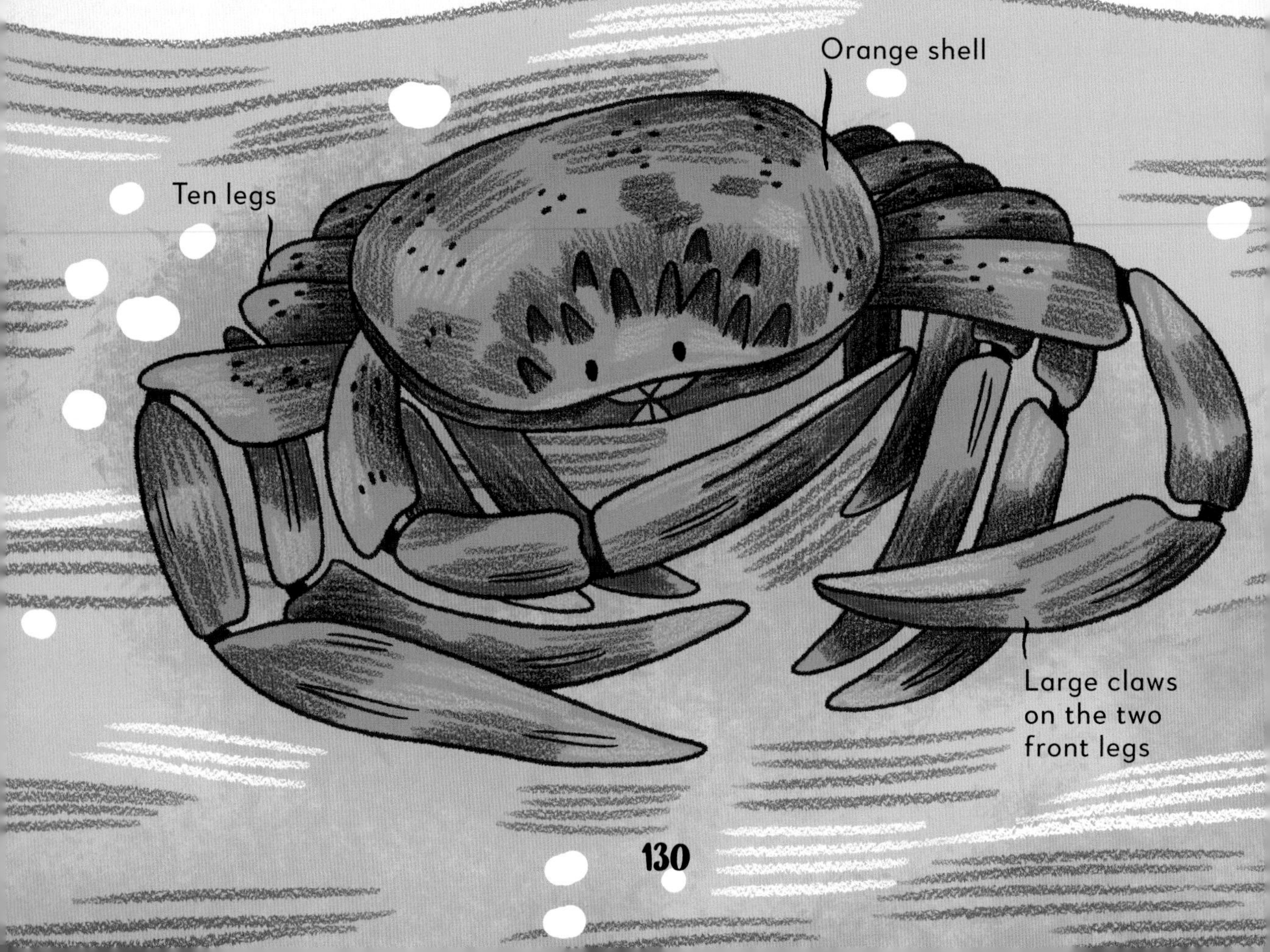

Orange shell

Ten legs

Large claws on the two front legs

Mantis shrimp

Mantis shrimp pack a fast **punch**! If another animal gets too close, they use their front legs to thump it.

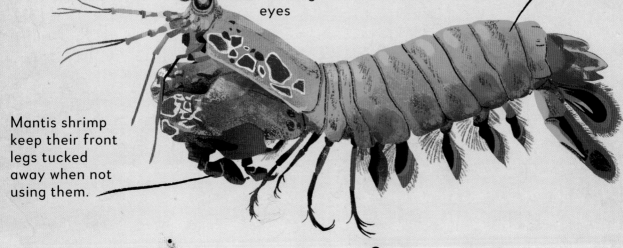

Bright green shell

Two huge eyes

Mantis shrimp keep their front legs tucked away when not using them.

Krill

Almost see-through body

Tiny legs

Two beady eyes

Krill live together in huge groups called swarms. Many krill can flash **lights** from their bodies to scare away predators.

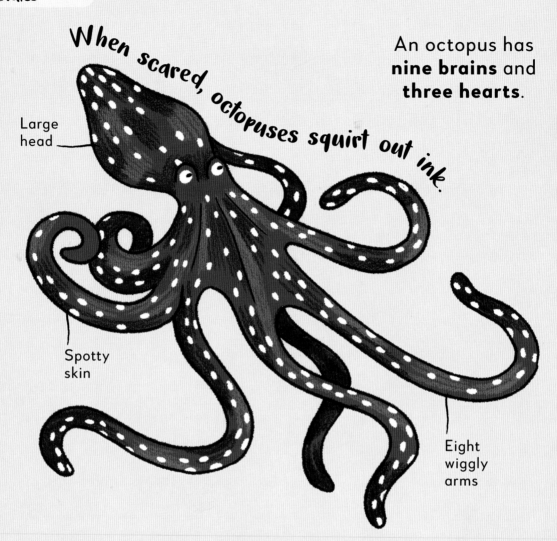

When scared, octopuses squirt out ink.

An octopus has **nine brains** and **three hearts**.

Large head

Spotty skin

Eight wiggly arms

Octopus

Wriggling, muscly octopuses swim through the water powered by their eight arms. Each arm has hundreds of sticky **suckers** that help the octopus to move around and to grab prey.

Cuttlefish

Long, flappy fin

This cunning creature would be great at hide-and-seek. It can **change** color to look like rocks or sand on the seabed!

These soft-bodied invertebrates are all types of mollusk.

Nautilus

The nautilus has almost one hundred arms, called **tentacles**. It stretches them out of its hard shell to catch food.

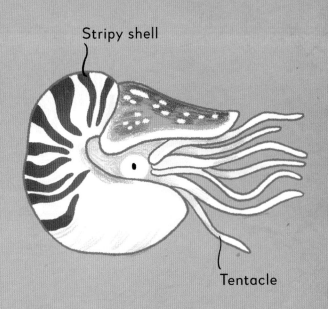

Stripy shell

Tentacle

All these animals are mollusks, too.

Snail

Snails can pull their bodies into their hard shells. They make **slime**, which they slide around on to move.

Spiral shell

Two antennae help slugs feel what is around them.

Slug

Slugs crawl by making wave movements with their **foot**. They live in damp places.

Foot

Smooth, gray skin

Mussel

Mussels live on sea shores. They **suck** in water to take tiny food out of it.

Each mussel is surrounded by two hard shells.

Nudibranch

These colorful sea slugs live on the **seabed**. They breathe through their skin or feathery gills.

Gills on back

Spotted, bumpy skin

Smooth, striped skin

Jellyfish

Squishy jellyfish have no brain, heart, bones, or eyes. They **drift** along with ocean currents.

A jellyfish's body is called a **bell**.

Arms with stingers

Sea pens **glow** in the dark when touched.

Branches of tentacles

Sea pen

Sea pens live on the seabed. They use their tentacles to catch food that is **floating** nearby.

Long stem

136

Anemone

Anemone live in **shallow** sea waters. They are not rooted in place, and can move across the seabed.

Tentacles hide an anemone's mouth.

Coral

Tropical waters are filled with beautiful groups of corals. These animals can form huge mounds called **reefs**.

Sticky tentacles for catching food

Extinct

Here are some of the many animals that once lived on Earth, but sadly no longer exist.

Triceratops was a plant-eating **dinosaur** with three long horns. It lived millions of years ago.

Horn

Thick tail

Triceratops

Curling **tusks**

Long **trunk**

This elephant-sized beast lived in ice-cold lands **thousands** of years ago. Mammoths were hunted by ancient humans.

Woolly mammoth

These **birds** were the size of a turkey. Humans hunted them, and the last dodo was seen in 1662.

Large beak

Dodo

Clawed feet

Endangered

There are only a small number of these animals left. They may become extinct very soon.

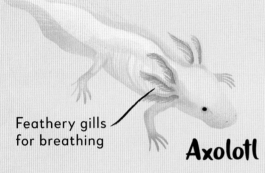

Axolotls now live in just a few lakes. **Dirty water** from a nearby city has made it hard for them to survive.

Feathery gills for breathing

Axolotl

No back fin

These porpoises are unusual because they live in a river. Many get caught in **fishing nets** by accident.

Yangtze finless porpoise

Horn

Javan rhinoceros

This is one of the **rarest** animals on Earth. There are only around sixty left. Each one has been given a name, to help us track and protect them.

Glossary

armor
Protective covering on an animal that keeps it from being harmed

backbone
Spine of an animal

blend
When an animal can match its surroundings

burrow
To dig down into the ground, or the hole where an animal lives

chrysalis
Stage of growth from caterpillar to butterfly

desert
Hot or cold place where not much rain falls

dorsal fin
Fin on the back of fish and marine mammals used for balance when swimming

grassland
Wide-open space covered by grass and flowers

habitat
Best place for specific animals to live. For example, sharks live in ocean habitats

lagoon
Area of shallow pond-like water

mollusk
Type of invertebrate with a soft body and, often, a hard shell

nectar
Sugary sweet liquid from a flower

nocturnal
Animals that sleep during the day and are awake at nighttime

poisonous
If something is poisonous, it contains poison—a substance that kills or damages living things

predator
Animal that hunts other animals

prey
Animal that is hunted by another animal

rainforest
Area with many trees where there is a large amount of rain

savanna
Large area of flat land with few trees, found in hot places

senses
Animal's view of the world using the five senses: sight, smell, taste, hearing, and touch

sensitive
When an animal can sense tiny things using its sense of touch

skeleton
Bony structure of an animal's body

transparent
See-through

tropical
Weather or habitat that is hot and damp

venom
Poisonous liquid

venomous
Animal that is able to pass on venom through a bite or sting

waterproof
Something that does not let water in. For example, skin is waterproof

wetland
Area of wet, muddy land where plants grow

wild
Where an animal lives free in the world

Animal A-Z

Author Zeshan Akhter
Illustrators Jean Claude, Livi Gosling, Kaja Kajfez, Charlotte Milner, Marc Pattenden, Sandhya Prabhat, Kate Slater, Sara Ugolotti

Editor Katie Lawrence
US Senior Editor Shannon Beatty
US Editor Mindy Fichter
Designer Sonny Flynn
Senior Designer and Jacket Designer Elle Ward
Editorial Assistant Kieran Jones
Design Assistants Sif Nørskov, Holly Price
Publishing Coordinator Issy Walsh
Managing Editor Jonathan Melmoth
Managing Art Editor Diane Peyton Jones
Production Editor Dragana Puvacic
Production Controller Magdalena Bojko
Deputy Art Director Mabel Chan
Publishing Director Sarah Larter

Educational Consultant Penny Coltman

First American Edition, 2022
Published in the United States by DK Publishing
1450 Broadway, Suite 801, New York, NY 10018

A catalog record for this book
is available from the Library of Congress.
ISBN: 978-0-7440-5011-0

DK books are available at special discounts
when purchased in bulk for sales promotions, premiums,
fund-raising, or educational use. For details,
contact: DK Publishing Special Markets,
1450 Broadway, Suite 801, New York, NY 10018
SpecialSales@dk.com

Printed and bound in China

For the curious
www.dk.com

Acknowledgments

DK would like to thank: Helen Peters for the index and Caroline Hunt for proofreading.

Illustrations copyright © Charlotte Milner 2018:
11 Brown bear. 26 Brown bear. 122 Bumblebee. **Cover** Bumblebee.

Illustrations copyright © Sandhya Prabhat 2020:
69 Parrot. 73 Cockatoo. 72 Parrots. 91 Blue iguana. 95 Iguanas. **Cover** Parrots.

Illustrations copyright © Kate Slater 2020:
18–19 Dogs. 39 Giraffe. 52 Rabbit. 60–61 Anteater. 62–63 Elephants. 80 Andean condor, Red kite. 81 King vulture. 122 Fly, Flying ant. **Cover** Dog, Giraffe.

Illustrations copyright © Kate Slater 2022:
4–5 Tree of Life. 11 Mouse. 27 Polar bear. 53 Hares. 54–55 Rodents. 60–61 Sloth, Armadillo. 69 Bald eagle. 70–71 Songbirds. 81 Bald eagle, Peregrine falcon. 84 Flamingos. 85 Swans, Goose, Ducks. 109 Great white shark. 117 Sharks. 118 Praying mantis. 123 Praying mantis, Green lacewing, Wasp. **Cover** Flamingos.

All other images © Dorling Kindersley
For further information see www.dkimages.com